The · Life Cycle · Series

The Life Cycle of a
TREE

Bobbie Kalman & Kathryn Smithyman
Illustrations by Barbara Bedell
Crabtree Publishing Company
www.crabtreebooks.com

The Life Cycle Series
A Bobbie Kalman Book

Dedicated by Kathryn Smithyman
For Mum and Dad, who gave me roots

Editor-in-Chief
Bobbie Kalman

Writing team
Bobbie Kalman
Kathryn Smithyman
Niki Walker

Editor
Amanda Bishop

Cover and title page design
Campbell Creative Services

Computer design
Margaret Amy Reiach

Production coordinator
Heather Fitzpatrick

Photo researcher
Jaimie Nathan

Consultant
Patricia Loesche, Ph.D., Animal Behavior Program,
Department of Psychology, University of Washington

Photographs:
Robert McCaw: pages 13, 16 (bottom), 17 (both),
25 (top right)
Marc Crabtree: page 26 (top)
James Kamstra: page 27
Allen Blake Sheldon: page 18
Other images by Digital Stock, Digital Vision,
Corbis Images, and Adobe

Illustrations:
All illustrations by Barbara Bedell except
the following:
Margaret Amy Reiach: pages 9 (left), 14,
15 (top right), 18 (right), 20 (top left)
Bonna Rouse: pages 15 (bottom right), 22,
29 (bottom right), 31 (bottom right)
Antoinette "Cookie" Bortolon: pages 21 (top right),
22 (top), 23 (cone and seeds)
Tiffany Wybouw: pages 9 (top), 23 (top right)

Crabtree Publishing Company

www.crabtreebooks.com   1-800-387-7650

PMB 16A
350 Fifth Avenue
Suite 3308
New York, NY
10118

612 Welland Avenue
St. Catharines
Ontario
Canada
L2M 5V6

73 Lime Walk
Headington
Oxford
OX3 7AD
United Kingdom

Cataloging-in-Publication Data
Kalman, Bobbie
  The life cycle of a tree / Bobbie Kalman & Kathryn Smithyman;
illustrations by Barbara Bedell.
     p. cm. -- (The life cycle series)
Includes index.
Text and photographs describe basic facts about trees, their
function in a forest, and how they benefit animals, people,
and the environment.
  ISBN 0-7787-0689-3 (pbk.) -- ISBN 0-7787-0659-1 (RLB)
  1. Trees--Juvenile literature. 2. Trees--Life cycles--Juvenile
literature. [1. Trees.] I. Smithyman, Kathryn
II. Bedell, Barbara, ill. III. Title.
  QK475.8 .K36 2002
  582.16--dc21
                                                    LC 2002002279

Contents

What is a tree?

A tree is a living thing. It is a large green plant. Like all plants, trees make their own food from light, air, and water. Trees come in many shapes, colors, and sizes, but they have the same basic parts.

The parts of a tree

All trees have a trunk, branches, leaves, and roots. The trunk carries water and **nutrients**, or food, from the roots to the branches and leaves. It also carries the food made by the leaves to the rest of the tree. The parts of a tree may look different on various trees, but they do the same jobs.

*Leaves **absorb**, or take in, sunlight and make food for the tree.*

The roots hold the tree securely in the ground. They also draw water and nutrients out of the soil to nourish the tree.

Two types of trees

There are two main kinds of trees—**conifers** and **broadleafs**. Conifers are trees with needle-like leaves. They are called conifers because they grow woody cones. Pine, spruce, and fir trees are conifers. Broadleafs have flat, wide leaves with veins. Apple, oak, and maple trees are all broadleaved trees.

Where do trees grow?

*A **tropical rainforest** is a lush habitat. The warm, moist air provides perfect growing conditions for many species of trees.*

Trees grow almost everywhere in the world, but they cannot live in the far north or in Antarctica. Each **species**, or type, of tree can live only in certain **habitats**. A habitat is an area that receives a specific amount of sunlight and rainfall and has a certain type of soil. Habitats include forests, swamps, mountainsides, and deserts.

Trees do not grow on high mountain peaks. The temperature is too cold and there is not enough rain.

Cypress trees grow in swamps. Their "knees" help stabilize the trees and may also help them breathe.

Life in the cold

In areas where winter days are short and the weather is cold, broadleaved trees shed their leaves. As winter approaches, the leaves turn color, then fall to the ground. Shedding their leaves helps the trees save energy and keeps them from drying out. Without leaves, the trees become **dormant**, or inactive, until spring. Trees that shed their leaves for a season are called **deciduous** trees.

Coniferous trees

Coniferous trees grow well in parts of the world where winters are long and very cold. Their branches slope downward, so heavy snow slides off without breaking them. Their small leaves are not easily ripped off by strong winds, and the leaves have a waxy coating that keeps them from drying out.

*A few types of conifers are deciduous. Most are **evergreen**, however, which means they keep their leaves year-round.*

What is a life cycle?

Every living thing goes through a set of changes called a **life cycle**. A tree begins its life as a seed. The seed grows and changes until it becomes a fully grown tree. Some trees grow faster than others, but they all need several years to become **mature**. Mature trees are able to make seeds. When these seeds begin to grow, a new life cycle begins.

Life span

A **life span** is the length of time a tree lives. Many trees live for several hundred years. Some, such as the giant sequoia shown left, have life spans of several thousand years.

The life cycle of a tree

A tree's life cycle begins when a seed **germinates**, or begins to grow. Once a seed grows a tiny root and **stem**, it is called a **seedling**. As its stem grows bigger and its leaves form, the seedling becomes a **sapling**, or a very young tree.

A sapling's stem begins to turn woody, and it continues growing branches and leaves. It takes many years of growing before the sapling develops into a mature tree. Once the tree is mature, it can make seeds to produce new trees.

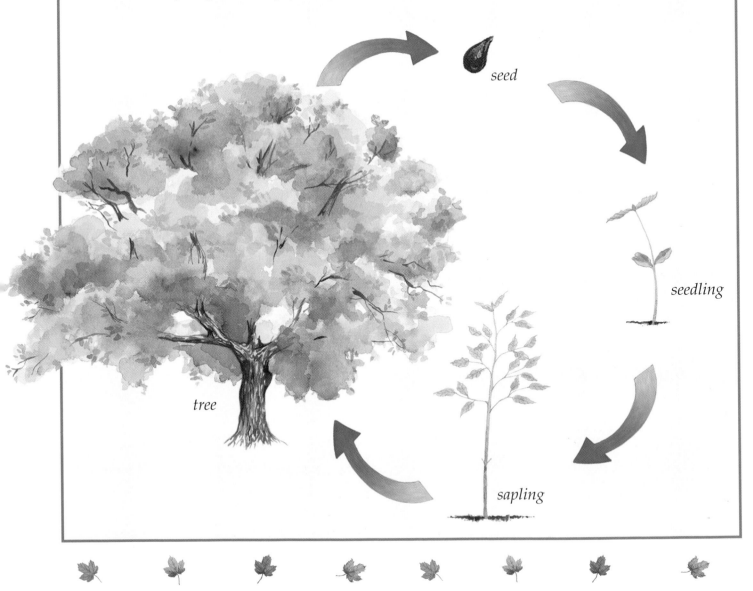

seed

seedling

sapling

tree

Growing from a seed

No matter how big it might grow, every tree begins its life as a seed. A seed contains an **embryo**, or tiny unformed tree. It also holds a store of food that the embryo lives on until it can start making its own food. Seeds do not always start growing right away. They need a certain amount of heat and water before they can start to germinate. Seeds stay dormant until conditions are just right for them to grow. Many seeds are tough enough to survive months of **drought** or cold weather. Some seeds can stay dormant for years!

Germination

When a seed has the right conditions, it starts to take in water through a tiny hole in its **seed coat**. Germination has begun! Depending on its size, a seed can take days or months to finish germinating.

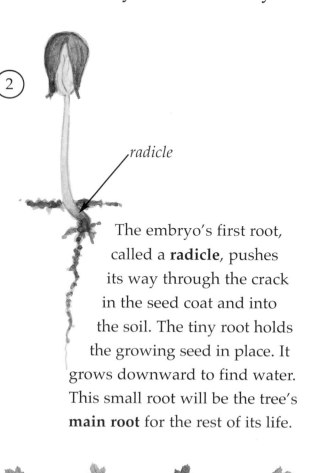

②

radicle

①

seed coat

The tiny embryo absorbs water and swells until it cracks its tough seed coat.

The embryo's first root, called a **radicle**, pushes its way through the crack in the seed coat and into the soil. The tiny root holds the growing seed in place. It grows downward to find water. This small root will be the tree's **main root** for the rest of its life.

Some like it hot

Fire helps make conditions right for some seeds to germinate. In forests where there is too little space and sunlight for new plants to grow, fire clears the way. Some conifer seeds stay sealed in their cones until the heat of a fire opens the cones. Other seeds need the heat from a fire to crack their tough seed coats.

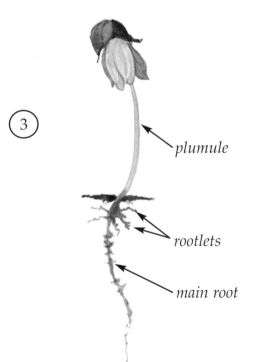

③ *plumule*

rootlets

main root

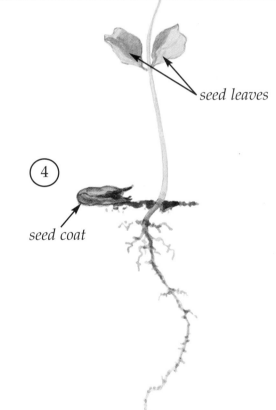

④ *seed leaves*

seed coat

The first shoot, called the **plumule**, starts to push its way up toward sunlight. Small hairlike roots, called **rootlets**, grow out from the main root. Over time, they will grow and branch out into a network of roots.

Finally, the **seed leaves** push their way out of the seed coat, which falls away. The short, stubby seed leaves do not look like the leaves of a grown tree. They contain food, which the tiny plant uses to keep growing.

Seedling to sapling

After a seed germinates and its seed leaves emerge, the tiny tree is called a seedling. Using the food from its seed leaves, the seedling grows quickly. Before long, a new shoot begins to grow between the seed leaves. This slim green stem will become the tree's trunk. The seedling's first **true leaves** will grow from the stem a few weeks later. The true leaves are the same shape as those of an adult tree, but they are not as big.

Small and green

During the summer, the seedling grows taller and thicker. It also adds more leaves to its stem. When summer ends, the seedling stops growing. It is now about a foot (30 cm) tall. The seedling will start growing again the following spring.

Photosynthesis

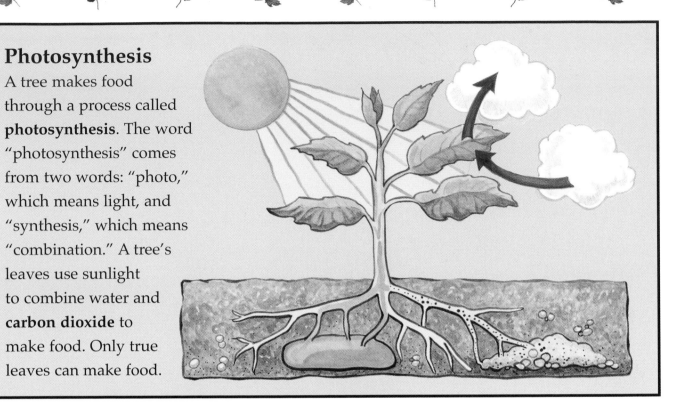

A tree makes food through a process called **photosynthesis**. The word "photosynthesis" comes from two words: "photo," which means light, and "synthesis," which means "combination." A tree's leaves use sunlight to combine water and **carbon dioxide** to make food. Only true leaves can make food.

Not all seedlings survive to be saplings. This birch seedling germinated in the crack of a rock. Its roots may not be able to spread enough to support the tiny tree.

On its way

After a few years of growing, the young tree looks like a small copy of its parent tree. It is now called a sapling. Most saplings are between three and six-and-a-half feet (1-2 m) tall. Their thick, woody stems help support many branches and leaves.

Growing up and out

A sapling does most of its growing in the spring and summer. It grows two ways—up and out. Its trunk, roots, and branches grow longer, making the tree taller and wider. The tree's parts also get heavier as they grow. Its trunk, roots, and branches must grow thicker as they get longer to hold up the weight of the tree.

Tall and wide

The top four feet (1.2 m) of soil contain many nutrients, so tree roots usually stay there. As roots grow, they spread out rather than pushing farther down to form a wide base for the tree. A wider base helps keep the tree from toppling over as it grows.

Branching out

Branches grow short thin shoots called **twigs**. Each spring, twigs grow out of buds. Every twig has a **leading bud** on its tip. The shoot in the leading bud grows to add length to the twig. The leading bud also contains leaves. **Lateral buds** grow from the side of each twig and cause the twigs to branch out.

leading bud

lateral buds

The branch grows in length from the leading bud. Twigs on the side of the branch grow from the lateral buds.

Crowning glory

A young tree grows taller mainly by adding to the top of its trunk. Its branches do not grow as quickly as its trunk, so the tree looks cone-shaped. A conifer usually keeps this shape, but a broadleaved tree does not. When a broadleaf becomes mature, it does not add much to its height. Instead, it grows more branches. The branches grow longer and fuller, making the tree's **crown**, or top, more rounded in shape.

Every year, a tree adds a new ring to its trunk. Each ring is made up of a dark and a light layer. The dark part forms in the spring and the light part grows in the summer. You can tell a tree's age by counting its rings.

15

Mature trees

A tree becomes mature when it can reproduce by making seeds. Trees grow flowers in order to make seeds. Flowers come in all shapes, sizes, and colors.

Most broadleaved trees make colorful flowers called **blossoms**. Others have clusters of tiny flowers. Several trees, such as the one on the left, have flowers that look like tassels.

Inside a blossom

Flowers have special parts that they use to make seeds. Most broadleaved trees grow this type of blossom, which contains all the parts in a single flower. Blossoms, shown right, have **stamens** which produce **pollen**. Inside, each blossom has tiny **ovules**, which need pollen in order to become seeds. Some broadleafs grow two types of flowers. One type, called the male, produces the pollen. The other flower, called the female, contains the ovules.

Stamens produce tiny sticky grains of pollen.

*The ovules, which are hidden in the **ovary** at the base of the **pistil**, form the seeds.*

To catch pollen, these female pine flowers grow upright from their branches.

Conifer "flowers"

Like some broadleafs, a mature conifer tree produces male and female flowers. Each male flower produces pollen, and each female flower is designed to catch it. Conifer flowers have the same parts as broadleaf flowers, but they are not true flowers. True flowers have their ovules inside, and conifer flowers have theirs on the outside.

Pollination

A bee flies from flower to flower in search of nectar. If it touches the stamens of a flower, pollen rubs off onto its body. When the bee flies to another flower and rubs against its pistil, that flower may be pollinated.

Flowers cannot make seeds until **pollination** occurs. Pollination is the movement of pollen from one flower to another. The pollen has to be from the same type of tree as that of the flower it reaches in order for pollination to happen. Pollen is spread in many different ways.

Animal attraction

Trees with blossoms are pollinated by animals that move from flower to flower. These animals are called **pollinators**. Pollinators are attracted to bright, sweet-smelling tree blossoms that contain a sugary liquid called **nectar**. Pollinators feed on nectar. Their bodies must rub against the blossom's pollen in order to reach the nectar. Pollen grains stick to their bodies and rub off on the other flowers they visit.

Blowing in the wind

All conifers rely on wind to spread their pollen, as do broadleaved trees with tassel-like flowers. Wind-pollinated flowers are not colorful or scented because they do not need to attract animals. Instead, they are shaped so that wind can easily sweep pollen off the male flowers and carry it to the female flowers.

Pollen from one of these conifers must reach the female flowers of another tree so that pollination can take place. Flowers on the same tree cannot pollinate one another.

Making seeds

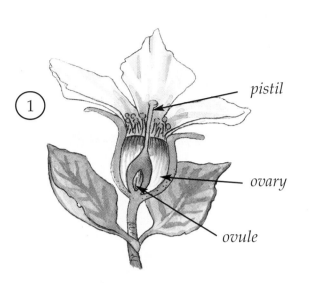

1

pistil

ovary

ovule

Once a blossom is pollinated, a seed begins to grow inside it. The blossom goes through a series of changes as the seed grows. The ovary grows around the seed and eventually becomes a protective case called a **fruit**.

*When pollen lands on the tip of the pistil, a tube forms and grows downward until it reaches the ovary. The pollen travels down the tube into the ovary and **fertilizes** the ovules so they can become seeds.*

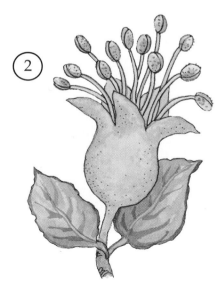

2

The blossom petals drop off and the stamens wither. The ovary begins to grow as seeds form inside the ovule.

3

The ovary continues to grow and thicken to protect the seeds growing inside.

4

This part of the apple was the ovary.

Finding the fruit

When people think of fruits, they usually imagine soft, juicy foods that are good to eat. Not all fruits are juicy, however, and not all can be eaten! Fruits are simply the parts of trees that contain seeds. Some fruits are the hard shells of seeds that we call "nuts." Others are dry, papery pods, such as the wings on a maple seed.

As the seeds grow, female conifer flowers harden and become cones. Pine cones stay closed until the seeds are formed.

As the seeds develop, the green pine cone becomes brown and woody.

Fleshy fruits such as this plum contain only one seed. Other fruits, such as apples, hold several seeds.

A walnut's hard outer shell is actually a fruit. The seed is the part of the nut that people eat.

A maple key has two seeds tucked inside.

Each seed inside a Douglas fir cone has a wing that sticks out of the cone.

Seeds on the move

When a bird, such as this parrot, eats small fruits, the seeds pass through its body. The seeds are dispersed in the bird's droppings.

Animals such as squirrels store food by burying nuts. If the nuts stay buried long enough, the seeds could take root and grow.

Seeds must reach soil in order to grow. They also need sunlight and space to grow after they germinate. The branches of parent trees block out sunlight, and their roots take most of the water and nutrients from the soil. For these reasons, seeds must move away from their parents to have a better chance of growing. The movement of seeds away from their parent trees is called **dispersal**.

Fruit and nuts

Seeds that are contained in fruits or nuts are dispersed by the animals that eat them. When an animal eats a fruit, it may swallow small seeds. Seeds that pass through the animal's body are released in the animal's droppings, often far away from the parent tree. Once the seed has reached the soil, it can begin growing.

Gone with the wind

A few broadleaved trees, such as maples, have seeds that are easily carried by the wind. When a maple seed is ready to grow, the dry pod breaks away from the tree.

The maple key's "wings" keep it from falling straight down. The key flutters on the wind until it finally falls to the ground. Some maple seeds are blown far from their parent trees.

Flying from cones

If a cone ripens and lets its seeds go when the wind is not blowing, the seeds simply fall to the ground beneath the parent tree, where they cannot grow. If a cone releases its seeds on a windy day, however, the seeds may be carried far enough from the parent to grow.

In the forest

In the wild, trees usually do not live alone. In open areas away from cities, towns, and farms, trees grow in forests, which are home to countless other plants and animals. More than half of all the plant and animal species in the world live in forests! Forest creatures rely on the trees, plants, and each other for survival. They form **food chains**. Some animals eat leaves, bark, sap, flowers, and fruits of trees. The animals may then be eaten by other creatures.

Fueling the forest

Even after a tree dies, it helps other living things in the forest. A dead tree soaks up water and slowly rots, becoming a perfect place for ferns, fungi, mosses, and seedlings to grow. Many insects live in the rotting tree, and birds feed on the insects. If the dead tree falls to the ground, it often becomes a shelter for toads, worms, salamanders, snails, and beetles.

Forming a forest

Forests form slowly over hundreds of years. The first trees to grow are trees that need plenty of room and sunlight. These trees are called **pioneers**. Over time, the seeds of trees that grow well in shade take root near the pioneers. As more kinds of trees grow, animals begin to make their homes in the forest.

Forests are home to many kinds of trees in different stages of their life cycles.

Threats to trees

Trees face a number of dangers, including insect pests, forest fires, and diseases. The biggest threat to trees and forests, however, is people.

Acid rain

Acid rain damages huge areas of forests in North America and in parts of Europe. It is caused when air pollution from cars and factories mixes with water droplets in clouds and then falls as rain or snow. Acid rain harms tree leaves, often causing them to fall off. Without leaves, the trees can no longer make food and they die. Acid rain also makes the soil around tree roots toxic. Old trees are damaged and new trees cannot take root.

When camping, ask a ranger if campfires are permitted. In dry weather, they may not be. If fires are allowed, build them only in proper fire pits or designated areas.

*Asian longhorned beetles pose a threat to trees in Chicago and New York City. They came to North America with goods shipped from Asia. They have no natural **predators** here. They eat the trees, but nothing eats them.*

Disappearing forests

People have cleared more than half of the world's forests. Forests continue to disappear. An area the size of a football field is cut down every second! In North America, only a few **old growth** forests remain. In South America, enormous areas of rainforest are **clear-cut** every day so the land can be used for ranching and building. When a forest is clear-cut, every part of it is cut or burned to the ground, but only a few of the trees are actually used. Losing a large area of forest affects the temperature and the amount of rainfall in that area and even in other parts of the world. The area may become a desert where plants and animals can no longer survive.

*Some logging companies now use **selective logging**. They cut down only mature trees and leave younger trees to finish growing. Some also use **reforestation**. They plant new trees, but it takes a long time for these trees to grow, and the new forest does not have the variety of trees found in the old forest.*

How trees help us

How many times today did you use something that came from a tree? Trees give us foods such as fruits, nuts, cocoa, and maple syrup. Many important medicines also come from trees. Trees even help us breathe by adding **oxygen** to the air and removing carbon dioxide.

Important to the Earth

Trees shelter people and animals from the sun and wind. Their roots hold **topsoil** in place so that it is not **eroded**, or carried away by wind or water. Their trunks, leaves, and roots store water and keep soil from drying out. Trees prevent the land around them from becoming a desert.

*(left) Fallen leaves rot and break down into a soft, dark material called **humus**, which is full of the nutrients that plants need in order to grow.*

How we can help trees

The more you know about trees, the more you can do to help them. Learning about trees is a great first step, but there is much more you can do.

Think green

You can help reduce acid rain by convincing your family to drive less. Walk, ride your bike, or use public transit whenever you can. When your family does need to take a car, combine errands into one trip.

Family tree

Make a tree a part of your family! Plant a tree in your yard or a park. Give it a name and watch it grow. You can also raise money to adopt part of the rainforest. Your money will help protect hundreds or even thousands of trees!

Paper is precious

You can cut down on the amount of paper you use by:

- using both sides of your writing and computer paper
- using cloth napkins
- recycling your family's paper, newspapers, and boxes
- buying products made from recycled paper

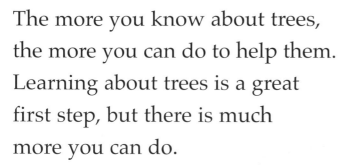

Learn more!

Send e-mail or letters to government officials asking them to protect threatened forests in your state or province. You can learn more about protecting all trees and forests by logging onto these Internet sites: www.forests.org, www.arborday.org, and www.rainforest-alliance.org.

Amazing trees!

Trees are amazing plants! It is hard to imagine our world without them. Some trees live to be ancient giants. Others live in such harsh conditions that it is hard to believe they are able to survive. Many trees survive by **adapting** to a changing world. Some can even grow new branches that repel the insect and animal predators that try to eat them.

Some redwoods grow to be more than 300 feet (91 m) tall and 18 feet (5.5 m) wide. There is a sequoia in California's Prairie Creek Redwoods State Park that is believed to be 12,000 years old. Now that's a big old tree!

Getting to know you!

Learn about the special things some trees can do and conduct your own tree study. Make "bark rubbings" of several trees to see if their bark is the same. Hold a piece of paper against a tree trunk and rub a crayon up and down the page until patterns appear. Compare the bark patterns of the trees you are studying. Then draw pictures of the branches of the same trees. How are they different? Choose one tree and measure its trunk at different times of the month. Is it always the same size? Stand with your back to a tree and feel the tree's energy. How does it make you feel?

Shrink and swell

Scientists have discovered that trees swell and shrink with the moon's rhythm in a way that is similar to the way the moon causes tides in oceans.

Spread the warning!

When giraffes on the African savannah feed on acacia leaves, the leaves send out a warning to the rest of the tree. Within a half hour, all the leaves of that tree, as well as those of nearby acacia trees, secrete bitter liquids called **tannins**. The giraffes are forced to stop eating them and move away to find other food.

Thirsty trees

The baobab tree, which grows in Africa and northern Australia, can hold up to 200 gallons (1000 liters) of water in its trunk!

Living off other trees

There are so many trees in a rainforest that some have adapted ways to force their way into an area. The strangler fig, shown right, is a **parasitic** tree. If its seed lands on another tree, called a **host**, it is able to germinate there rather than needing to reach the ground. As the fig sapling grows on the branch of the host, its roots slowly wind their way around the tree toward the ground. Once the strangler fig is anchored, its roots and branches surround the host and eventually kill it.

Glossary

Note: Boldfaced words that are defined in the book may not appear in the glossary

adapt To change in order to become better suited to the environment

carbon dioxide A gas, made up of carbon and oxygen, that is present in the air

drought A long period with no rainfall

fertilize To add pollen to an ovule in order to form a seed

food chain A pattern of eating and being eaten; for example, a plant is eaten by a rabbit that is then eaten by a fox

nectar A sweet liquid inside the flowers of various plants

old growth Describing a forest made up of mature trees and plants

oxygen A gas in the air that humans and animals need to breathe

parasitic Describing a plant or animal that lives and feeds on or inside another living thing

pollen A powdery substance produced by the stamens of flowers in order to create new flowers

predator An animal that hunts and eats other animals

reforestation The process of planting trees to replace forests that have been cut down

stamen The part of a flower that produces pollen

topsoil The top layer of soil

tropical rainforest Any forest near the equator that receives a lot of rain

Index

1 2 3 4 5 6 7 8 9 0   Printed in the U.S.A.   1 0 9 8 7 6 5 4 3 2